COPING

FAKE NEWS AND DISINFORMATION

ROBIN BAUSER

ROSEN PUBLISHING

Published in 2023 by The Rosen Publishing Group, Inc.
2544 Clinton Street, Buffalo, NY 14224

First Edition

Designer: Rachel Rising
Editor: Corona Brezina

Cataloging-in-Publication Data

Names: Bauser, Robin
Title: Fake news and disinformation / Robin Bauser.
Description: New York : Rosen, 2023. | Series: Coping|
Includes bibliographic references, index and glossary.
Identifiers: ISBN 9781499473650 (pbk) | ISBN 9781499473667
(library bound) | ISBN 9781499473674 (ebook)
Subjects: LCSH: Fake News--Juvenile literature. | Journalism
--Juvenile literature. | News Media-- Juvenile literature
Classification: LCC PN4784.F27 B38 2023 | DDC 070.9--dc23

Manufactured in the United States of America

CPSIA Compliance Information: Batch# CWRYA23. For further information contact Rosen Publishing at 1-800-237-9932.

CONTENTS

CHAPTER 1

STARTING UP THE PRESS

Fake news is making real headlines today. Fake news is inaccurate information that can spread across social media and other digital platforms, potentially misleading people on critical issues related to current events. It's easy to share fake news unwittingly, especially when you agree with the general gist of the story. But when enough people spread fake news, it can undermine trust in democratic institutions and cause people to base important decisions on false claims.

Disinformation is false information that is intended to mislead. People and organizations that produce disinformation know that it's not true. Another type of inaccurate information is misinformation, which isn't necessarily intended to mislead. Misinformation may start as a rumor that spreads without people bothering to check or verify whether the claim is true.

Fake news might seem like a 21st-century crisis, but it's actually nothing new. Since the very invention of mass media over 500 years ago, governments and people have debated and clashed over what type of information is appropriate for public consumption.

INVENTING THE PRESS

Johannes Gutenberg changed the world. Prior to Gutenberg's invention of the printing press in the mid-15th century, the reproduction of books, pamphlets, and other media was most often done by hand. Books were in short supply, and with few books, few people were able to read. At the time of the printing press's invention, just 30 percent of Europeans were literate.

Johannes Gutenberg invented the printing press in Germany around 1450, ushering in an information revolution that enabled mass publication of books and other print media.

Before Gutenberg invented the printing press, books had to be laboriously copied by hand, making them luxury items available only to the wealthy.

The automation provided by Gutenberg's printing press led to the release of more books, pamphlets, and other media. Three centuries after the printing press's invention, the U.S. Constitution was signed, and 60 percent of the new country's free adult population was literate. In 2017, the UNESCO (United Nations Educational, Scientific and Cultural Organization) Institute for Statistics (UIS) reported that 99 percent of adults in Europe and North America were literate; the global adult literacy rate was 86 percent.

Gutenberg's invention laid the groundwork for generations of technologies that would continue to improve access to information, including typewriters, copy machines, and computers. The printing press also enabled the development of journalistic print media—later to include radio, television, and the internet—that collectively became known as "the press."

LIMITING THE PRESS

When technologies emerge, governments often debate what regulations should be enacted, determining who can use the new technology, how the new technology can be used, and when the new technology can be used.

In the 17th century, one way the press in the United Kingdom—and later the British colonies in North America—was regulated was through licensing. In accordance with the Licensing Act, before any book or pamphlet could be printed, it had to first be registered with the Stationers' Company, a government-approved guild of printers. (The Stationers' Company is still in existence today, with over 900 members who represent press organizations, as well as paper, print, publishing, and office products companies.)

The Licensing Act—which would go through periods of renewal and lapse in 1695—did not eliminate press freedom in the United Kingdom, but it did limit it. Preventing someone from writing or saying something in advance is known as "prior restraint." Prior restraint was an issue of debate for the Founding Fathers as they tackled freedom of the press and freedom of speech in the U.S. Constitution. If something the government found objectionable did manage to be licensed and published, laws were enacted that could be used to limit the press after the fact.

PUBLISHING IN THE AMERICAS

North America's first printing press arrived in the Massachusetts Bay Colony in 1638. Colonial governments enforced the British press licensing law. With the final lapse of the Licensing Act in the late 17th century, local colonial governments debated implementing their own licensing laws. The colonial American press ultimately remained free from licensing restrictions in the 18th century, but it could still have its ability to publish limited by libel laws.

One of America's best-known libel trials occurred decades before the country gained its independence. The case of *Crown v. John Peter Zenger* was heard in 1735. Upset with the critical coverage he was receiving in the *New-York Weekly Journal*, New York governor William Cosby and his administration sought to charge not the newspaper's editors with seditious libel—publishing malicious content about the government—but to instead charge John Peter Zenger, the paper's printer, in an effort to shut the paper down. The validity of the statements made in the paper did not matter. The question of the case was whether Zenger published those statements or not. Zenger won his case and was found not guilty by a jury and returned to printing.

The U.S. Constitution was shaped by this history, with the Founding Fathers valuing the flow of information and the ability of citizens to criticize their government, but also seeing value in placing some limits on the press. From this came

During his 1735 trial for libel, John Peter Zenger was defended by Andrew Hamilton, who won a key early victory for the freedom of the press with the case.

the First Amendment of the U.S. Constitution, ratified in 1791, which states, “Congress shall make no law respecting an establishment of religion, or prohibiting the free exercise thereof; or abridging the freedom of speech, or of the press; or the right of the people peaceably to assemble, and to petition the government for a redress of grievances.”

Though it established an independent press in the United States—meaning a press not operated or controlled by the government—the First Amendment did not protect the press from any and all limitations. The first restriction came with the Sedition Act of 1798, which made it illegal to write or say something false, scandalous, or malicious against the government. People were jailed for violating the act before it expired in 1801.

Members of the press are prohibited from writing (libel) or saying (slander) anything knowingly false about a person and can be sued for the false statements they report. The government can request a story not be published or aired if it threatens national security. Journalists can be asked to turn over their notes or reveal their sources if they have information that could impact national security or public safety, such as witnessing a crime while reporting a story. Publications can challenge these requests in court, citing the First Amendment protection of the press, a protection few other occupations enjoy in the United States.

In Canada, Section 2 of the Canadian Charter of Rights and Freedoms, enacted in 1982, established that country’s independent press. It reads, “Everyone has the following fundamental freedoms: (a) freedom of conscience and religion;

Freedom of the press and freedom of speech are guaranteed in the U.S. Constitution, but there are restrictions, such as laws against libel and slander.

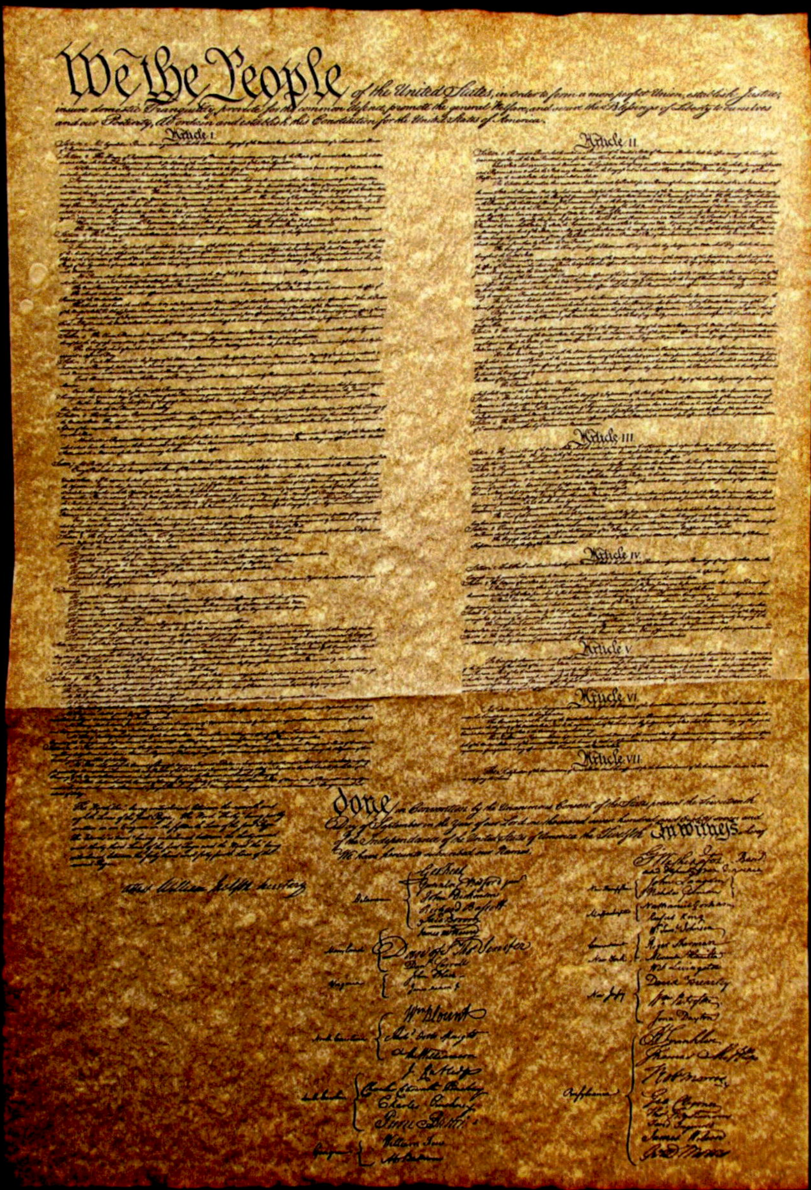

(b) freedom of thought, belief, opinion and expression, including freedom of the press and other media of communication; (c) freedom of peaceful assembly; and (d) freedom of association."

Like their counterparts in the United States, Canadian journalists can also be subject to libel or slander complaints and may be required by the government to turn over their reporting notes or reveal their sources. Freedom House, an independent watchdog organization that monitors and reports on challenges to freedom around the world, rated the press in both the United States and Canada as "free" in its "Freedom of the Press 2017" report. The organization reported just 13 percent of the world's population lived in countries with a free press.

Today, the freedom of speech guaranteed by the First Amendment of the Constitution largely protects the circulation of fake news stories and other types of disinformation in the U.S. Although certain forms of harmful expression are restricted, false statements and offensive speech such as racist statements and statements promoting violence cannot be outlawed. Social media companies can police the discourse on their platforms, but the First Amendment protects the opinions of social media users from government censorship.

The framers of the Constitution could never have imaged today's fake news climate. Fake news is produced and spread by foreign powers such as Russia, Iran, and China. Disinformation is posted and shared by social media accounts belonging to bots rather than actual users. Fake news can even be created by artificial intelligence.

A 2019 survey found that 73 percent of Americans agreed that people from opposing political backgrounds couldn't even agree on basic facts. Fake news is at least partially responsible for the divide.

Fake news has contributed to a partisan divide in the U.S. and has left many people skeptical of news stories from reputable news sources.

THE BIG LIE

One of the most notorious fake news narratives is the "Big Lie." This is the claim by former President Donald Trump and his followers that the 2020 election was "stolen." Believers in the "Big Lie" contend that President Joe Biden's win was the result of voter fraud.

On January 6, 2021, a mob of Trump supporters stormed the U.S. Capitol in Washington, D.C., in an attempt to prevent certification of the election results. The attackers interrupted the session of Congress, fought with police, and caused about $1.5 million in damage to the building. Biden was confirmed as president later in the evening after rioters dispersed.

Official election reviews and numerous investigations found no evidence of widespread voter fraud in the 2020 election. Nonetheless, the "Big Lie" persisted long after Biden's inauguration. Trump supporters continued to put forth claims of voting fraud. One year after the insurrection, nearly a quarter of Americans believed that Biden's victory was "definitely not legitimate." In early 2022, a significant number of candidates running for office in midterm elections across the country were election deniers.

On January 6, 2021, lawmakers hid or evacuated the building as rioters pushed through barriers, battled with police, and stormed the U.S. Capitol.

CHAPTER 2

COVERING THE NEWS

Print newspapers and magazines are in a state of decline. The rise of the internet provided many people with an alternate source for their news. The adoption of cell phones created a new distraction for moments when they may otherwise have been reading a newspaper, magazine, or book. As subscription numbers dropped, advertisers followed people to online outlets. Advertisement revenue for newspapers fell, causing financial turmoil and layoffs in the industry. According to *Forbes*, the number of people working for newspapers dropped from 74,410 in 2006 to 30,820 in 2020. Many small newspapers have shut down, and others have been bought by larger news organizations and consolidated under new ownership.

These trends have created "news deserts" across the country that lack any comprehensive and unbiased source of community news. For some people, social media has filled the gap. But newspapers maintain journalistic standards regarding accuracy, accountability, and fairness, whereas social media posts generally make no claim of impartiality. In losing newspaper reporting, the public loses watchdogs who help keep the powerful accountable to the public.

The situation was very different in the 19th century, when newspapers were widely read but journalistic standards were looser. As the United States expanded westward, eventually stretching from the Atlantic coast to the Pacific, so, too, did the country's press grow. Newspapers provided the growing nation's people with information on the wars, discoveries, and tragedies that would define their time in history.

In the early 20th century, most large cities had multiple newspapers with large circulation numbers, some of which printed more than one edition every day.

Nellie Bly's reporting, which appeared in Joseph Pulitzer's *New York World* newspaper in 1887, helped lead to major reforms at the New York City Lunatic Asylum.

Like the media of today, 19th-century newspapers covered current events but also featured in-depth reporting on major societal issues. One example was the undercover reporting done by Elizabeth Cochrane Seaman (using her pen name Nellie Bly) at the New York City Lunatic Asylum on Blackwell's Island in New York. Cochrane posed as a patient to gather firsthand accounts of the mistreatment experienced by patients at the facility.

STORIES AND SENSATIONALISM

While providing American readers with news, information, and opinion in their papers, many publishers also ran incredibly successful businesses. Publishers like Pulitzer and William Randolph Hearst gained power and built fortunes operating papers in cities throughout the United States. Filling their pages with sensational stories of local crime and international strife, these publishers were able to influence government policy and sell a lot of newspapers. This type of journalism came to be known as "yellow journalism," named for the character in a popular comic strip that ran first in Pulitzer's *New York World* and then in Hearst's *New York Journal*.

After nearly 400 years of Spanish colonial rule, Cubans were fighting for their independence in the late 1800s. Many in the United States backed this growing revolution, including Pulitzer and Hearst. Their newspapers featured articles about what was occurring in Cuba, even if they didn't always have reporters on the ground to cover the events. The stories weren't always accurate, but the vivid war coverage sold a lot of papers for the publishers.

The newspapers openly supported the Cuban revolutionaries, as did their reporters. Reporters would bring medicine and rum to gain access to fighters. One reporter helped a teenager accused of incitement break out of jail and escape to the United States. The U.S. government was not yet convinced to get involved and wage war on Spain. The government did, however, display its military might in the region. The battleship *Maine* was sent to Havana as part of this effort. On February 15, 1898, the battleship sunk in the Havana harbor following an explosion. More than 225 Americans were killed. Debate flourished over the cause of the explosion. The newspapers quickly placed the blame on Spain, and the dramatic news stories helped rouse public support for war.

Soon after, the United States entered into the Spanish-American War and won. Spain gave up control over Cuba. The United States also gained control over Guam, Puerto Rico, and the Philippines.

During the Cuban War of Independence, Hearst sent a ceremonial sword with a diamond-studded ivory handle to the rebel commander, General Máximo Gómez, to smooth over access for his reporters.

WILLIAM RANDOLPH HEARST

MANIPULATING THE PUBLIC

Pulitzer and Hearst were far from the first people to spread exaggerated or false stories for political purposes. Fake news has long been employed to provoke reactions, stir up prejudice, and even promote violence. In the 15th century, a toddler went missing in Trento, Italy, and a preacher blamed members of the local Jewish community for the disappearance. He claimed that the child was murdered and his blood drained and drunk as part of a Passover celebration. The account spread, leading to the arrest and torture of members of Trento's Jewish community. Fifteen people were found guilty of the child's murder and were burned at the stake.

During the American Revolution, false reports were spread to increase support for the fight for independence. News was spread that the United Kingdom had enlisted Native Americans and foreign soldiers to join its fight against the American revolutionaries. In the 1800s, before the start of the Civil War, stories were spread about slave uprisings and crimes committed by slaves to turn public opinion against African Americans, with violent results.

A LEGACY OF BIAS

In their coverage of Cuba and the Spanish-American War, the Pulitzer and Hearst papers openly showed their bias against Spain. Since the establishment of professional journalism schools at the turn of the 20th century, the ideal has been to strive for accurate, fair, and ethical reporting.

According to a 2021 Gallup poll, however, only 36 percent of respondents reported that they trust the television, radio, and print media. This number has been declining since Gallup began tracking attitudes toward the media in 1972. In the 1970s, 68 to 72 percent trusted the media.

Today, individuals and independent organizations have created lists and tools to help media consumers determine what biases do exist in the press. The company Ad Fontes Media, for example, assigns news sources a score on a chart that rates bias and reliability. Another example is AllSides, which uses its media bias rating system to classify the political views of news sources as leaning left, center, or right.

The best and worst of today's journalism comes from this history. Joseph Pulitzer's legacy exemplifies both. His publishing empire grew by selling sensational stories. He also championed excellence in journalism. Pulitzer's will made provisions for the creation of the Pulitzer

It's everyone's job to be discerning when choosing news sources, whether they're newspapers, television shows, or online news organizations.

Prize, which recognizes achievement in journalism, letters, drama, and music.

In his will, Joseph Pulitzer also granted Columbia University a $2 million endowment for the establishment of a journalism school and for the creation of scholarships. The first classes at the Columbia Journalism School were held in 1912, four years after Walter Williams started the School of Journalism at the University of Missouri. Williams, who served as the Missouri journalism school's founding dean, wrote the Journalist's Creed in 1914. It outlines eight beliefs for journalists to follow that profess the value of accuracy, fairness, and truth in journalism. The Missouri School of Journalism says this about Williams's creed on its website: "More than one century later, his declaration remains one of the clearest statements of the principles, values and standards of journalists throughout the world."

Today, the Pulitzer Prizes for journalism recognize the stories that represent the greatest achievements each year in serving the public through reporting. The *Washington Post*, for example, was recognized in 2022 for its coverage of the January 6, 2001, attack on the U.S. Capitol. Journalists at the *Tampa Bay Times* won the prize in investigative reporting for a series on dangerously toxic working conditions at a battery recycling plant.

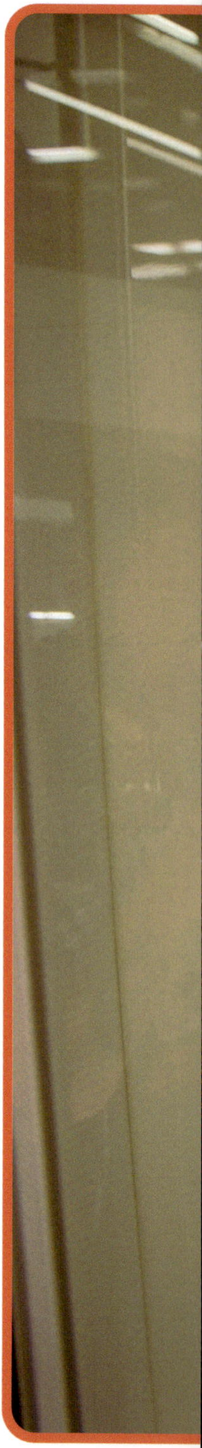

The Pulitzer Prize is the most prestigious honor in the field of journalism. Awards are presented in 14 categories, including investigative reporting, feature writing, editorial cartooning, and breaking news photography.

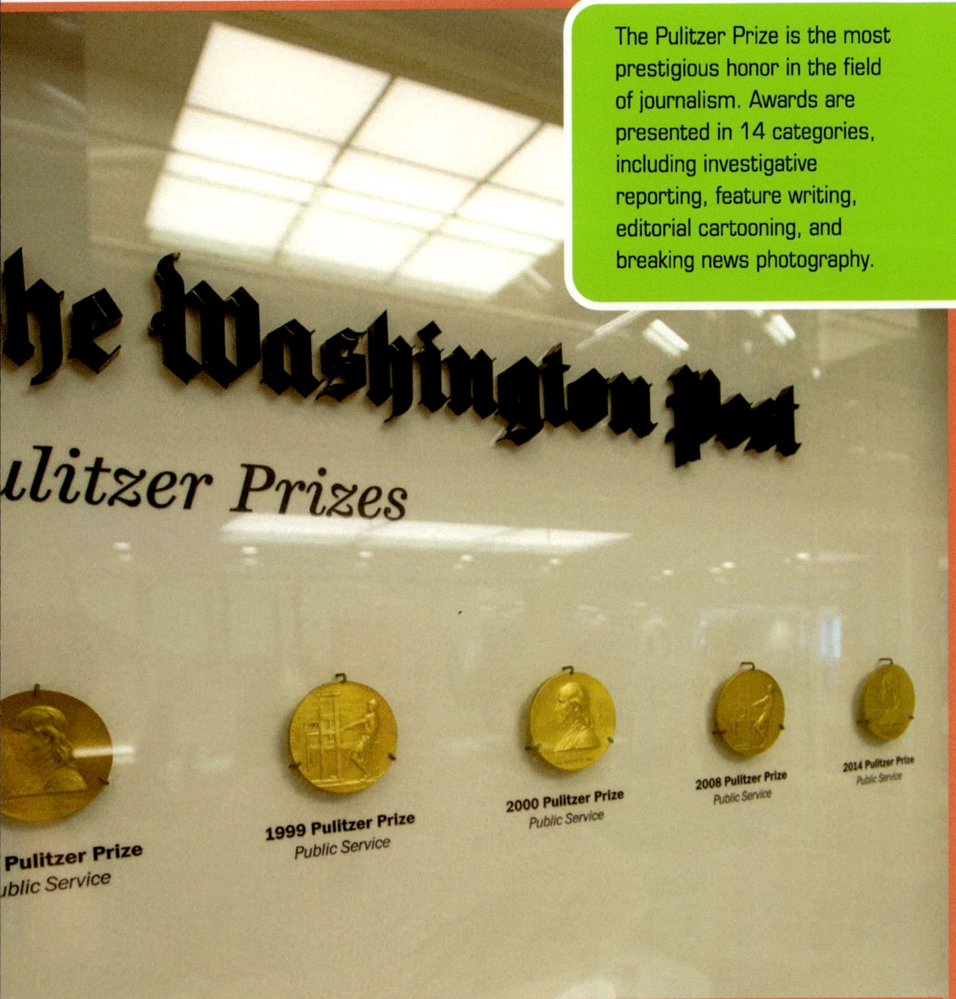

Social media allows users to spread news stories quickly, but platforms don't verify the quality or accuracy of the content.

There is no equivalent of the Pulitzer Prize for information shared on social media. It is possible that in time, new policies will hold users accountable for spreading fake news, just as newspapers made the transition away from sensationalism and exaggeration. In the meantime, stay skeptical and vigilant when consuming news from social media sources.

MYTHS & FACTS

MYTH: The media has a left wing bias.

FACT: A 2020 study published in the journal *Science Advances* found that there is no liberal bias regarding the stories that journalists choose to cover. More journalists do tend to lean liberal rather than conservative in their personal political views, but their own ideological bias does not affect their selection of topics to report in the news.

MYTH: No one reads newspapers anymore.

FACT: Although print circulation of newspapers has fallen, the number of users visiting newspapers' online websites has increased, according to a 2021 Pew Research Center fact sheet. The percentage of newspapers' digital advertising revenue has also risen.

MYTH: Fake news started because of social media.

FACT: Examples of deliberately false or exaggerated stories can be found throughout the history of print media. Social media, though, enables fake news to reach huge numbers of people very quickly.

CHAPTER 3

INVENTING THE NEWS

In June 2017, the *New York Times* published an editorial that linked a campaign ad for politician Sarah Palin to a mass shooting incident. The next day, the newspaper issued a correction, saying that some of the details in the story had been incorrect due to a mistake. Palin took the newspaper to court, claiming in a defamation lawsuit that the editorial had maliciously damaged her professional reputation. Attorneys for the paper argued that the editor had not knowingly or recklessly published false information. In 2022, the judge dismissed the case and the jury delivered a verdict against her.

The case demonstrates the levels of accountability in journalism—safeguards against fake news that don't exist on social media. If information is found to be incorrect in a published story, the paper issues a correction or retraction. If a journalist is found to have fabricated or plagiarized material, they are held accountable by the newspaper's editors. If someone believes that they have been defamed by the press, they have the recourse of taking the case to court.

Sarah Palin viewed her lawsuit against the *New York Times* as an attack by the "lamestream media." Other observers saw it as a challenge to the freedom of the press.

A PRIZE-WINNING LIE

Contemporary reporters who have been caught writing fake stories or using questionable sources were driven by various factors, from the pressure to succeed in a competitive industry to the desire to shine a spotlight on serious societal issues. Whatever their intentions, the publication of fabricated stories has consequences. Reporters and editors have lost their jobs. Newsroom practices are investigated and overhauled. Most damaging of all, the public can lose trust in the press.

Heroin was becoming a major issue in Washington, D.C., in the early 1980s, and reporters for the *Washington Post* were covering the crisis from a number of angles. Janet Cooke was one of these reporters. Originally from the Midwest and boasting an impressive résumé that included a Vassar College education, Cooke was assigned by her editor to investigate a new type of heroin. Though the young reporter was unable to track down the new drug, she learned quite a bit about heroin abuse in Washington, D.C., as later recounted in the April 19, 1981, article "The Players: It Wasn't a Game," written by *Washington Post* ombudsman Bill Green. Cooke also learned about children who were addicted to heroin.

From this investigation, the story "Jimmy's World" was born. Published on the front page of the *Post* on Sunday, September 28, 1980, the article told of an eight-year-old heroin addict who lived with his addict mother, identified as "Andrea," and her drug dealer boyfriend, identified as "Ron." Cooke recounted the boy's ambition to become a dealer himself one day and graphically described how Jimmy would be injected with heroin by his mother's boyfriend.

Even as Cooke was working on the story, people in the newsroom had their doubts, though concerns were not shared with top editors. Once the story

After her story was revealed to be fake, Cooke admitted she had inflated her résumé and her Pulitzer Prize nomination biography. She also confessed that Jimmy did not exist.

was published, law enforcement and local officials challenged it. Police searched for the boy but could not find him. Members of the *Post* staff searched for him unsuccessfully. But the *Post* was so confident in the story that it was submitted for a Pulitzer Prize.

Cooke was announced as the winner of the Pulitzer Prize for feature writing on April 13, 1981. Following this announcement, Jimmy's story started to unravel and, within two days of being awarded, Cooke returned the prize and the *Post* retracted the story. *Post* ombudsman Green conducted an investigation of Cooke and "Jimmy's World" for his article "The Players: It Wasn't a Game."

Prior to joining the *Post*, Cooke was a reporter for the *Toledo Blade*. The official biography of Cooke released by the Pulitzer Prize committee and carried by the Associated Press wire service did not match the information the *Blade* had about Cooke. The *Blade* contacted the Associated Press about the discrepancies, and the Associated Press contacted the *Post*. On April 16, 1981, the Post published an article by journalist David Maraniss, "The *Post* Reporter's Pulitzer Prize Is Withdrawn," as well a message to readers, "The End of the 'Jimmy' Story." In it, the paper's editors apologized to their readers and reflected on what went wrong. Green found blame throughout the *Post's* newsroom, including the editors who did not challenge Cooke's reporting and the reporters who did not bring up their concerns about Cooke's story to management.

A CLIMATE OF LIES

Climate change caused by human activities is leading to a warming world and disrupting the natural environment. Scientists have reached a consensus that climate change is real and driven by human beings. Nonetheless, fake media stories deny climate change and seek to discredit scientific research and policy measures implemented to curb climate change. For decades, the oil industry has spent millions of dollars attempting to cast doubt on climate change. Skeptics often oppose renewable energy initiatives with the claim that they would hurt the economy. A majority of Americans support prioritizing clean energy, but disinformation has contributed to the defeat of ambitious national policy measures to combat climate change.

Beginning in the 1970s, scientists working for the oil giant Exxon Mobil acknowledged the dangers of climate change even as the company misled the public on the issue in ads.

UNPROVEN ALLEGATIONS

In May 2014, the U.S. Department of Education's Office for Civil Rights released a list of 55 colleges and universities being investigated for how they handled sexual violence and harassment complaints. One of the schools on that list was the University of Virginia (UVA). When the list was published, a writer for *Rolling Stone* magazine was already working on an investigative feature about sexual violence on the campus and how campus administration dealt with those issues. Writer Sabrina Rubin Erdely connected with a UVA staff member seeking a case to include in the article. The staffer, a rape survivor who worked on campus as a sexual violence awareness specialist, knew a student on campus who might be willing to share her story.

Erdely first spoke with the student who would be known as "Jackie" in the article in July 2014—there were a total of eight interviews between July and October. Jackie described being assaulted at a fraternity party two years earlier by her date, an acquaintance, and several other unknown attackers. Those details became the focus of Erdely's article "A Rape on Campus: A Brutal Assault and Struggle for Justice at UVA," published in the November 19, 2014, issue of *Rolling Stone*.

Readers followed Jackie through the evening of the alleged attack, from her getting ready to be picked up by her date, who she only identified by first name to the writer, to her frantically calling her friends after her assault, who the writer did not interview.

The article followed Jackie as her friends tried to talk her out of filing charges, as she fell into depression, as she finally decided to go to campus administration with her story, and as she connected with a survivors' network on campus, naming the deans and advocates the anonymous Jackie met with. The article alleged that the university wasn't properly protecting students. Soon after Erdely's article was published, reporters from *Slate* and the *Washington Post* challenged its accuracy. The writer herself started having doubts about Jackie's story and *Rolling Stone* retracted the article. "A Rape on Campus" no longer appears on the *Rolling Stone* website; "An Anatomy of a Journalistic Failure," by Steve Coll, has taken its place. Erdely's original article can still be found online via web.archive.org.

Rolling Stone enlisted Steve Coll, dean of the Columbia Journalism School, to conduct an investigation into what went wrong during the publication process of "A Rape on Campus."

Coll and his collaborators on "An Anatomy of a Journalistic Failure," Sheila Coronel and Derek Kravitz, found:

> *Rolling Stone's* repudiation of the main narrative in "A Rape on Campus" is a story of journalistic failure that was avoidable. The failure encompassed reporting, editing, editorial supervision and fact-checking. The magazine set aside or rationalized as unnecessary essential practices of reporting that, if pursued, would likely have led the magazine's editors to reconsider publishing Jackie's narrative so prominently, if at all. The published story glossed over the gaps in the magazine's reporting by using pseudonyms and by failing to state where important information had come from.

The magazine also faced several lawsuits related to the article. Erdely was found responsible for defamation with actual malice against one of the deans named in the article, Nicole Eramo. *Rolling Stone* and parent company Wenner Media were also found responsible for defaming Eramo. The magazine reached a settlement with Phi Kappa Psi in its defamation case against *Rolling Stone*.

When editors find that they cannot stand behind the accuracy of a story, they may issue a retraction—a formal withdrawal of published material. Retractions are issued in serious cases. *Rolling Stone* removed the article "A Rape on Campus" from its archives. The story "Jimmy's World" remains in the online archive of the *Washington Post* accompanied by a statement that the article has been retracted.

Story corrections are more common than full retractions. Corrections are issued for errors such as misspelled proper names and incorrect facts and figures. Some publications also issue clarifications when a statement may be confusing or misleading but not factually incorrect. If a newspaper or magazine article, website, radio broadcast, or television show has incorrect information, a correction or retraction will be issued by the editors to acknowledge the error. A correction details what error was made, like misspelling a source's name, providing the wrong date for an event, or attributing a quote to the wrong person. For newspapers and magazines, the correction will appear in a later issue, identifying the article title and publication date, listing and correcting the error, and apologizing to readers for the error being made. Online, articles are updated to reflect the correction and an editor's note will appear with the article to let readers know changes have been made. Television and radio news programs may have a regularly scheduled time slot for reporting their corrections.

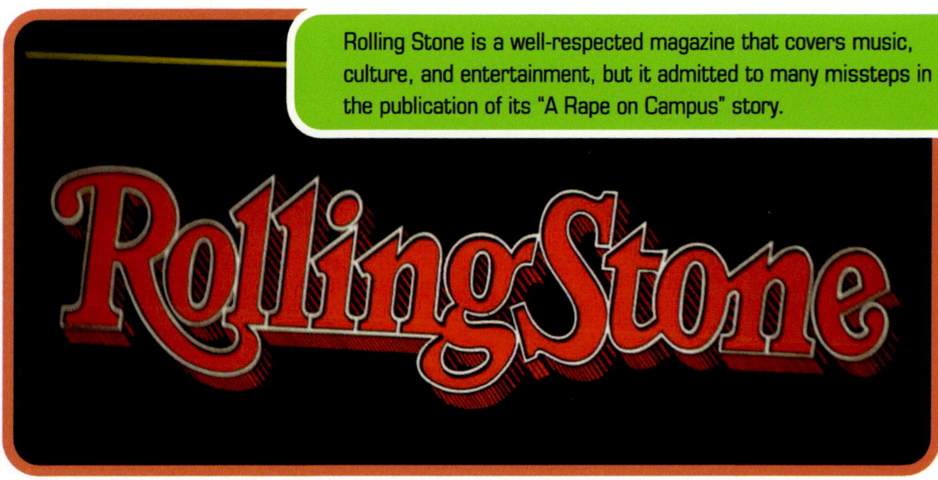

Rolling Stone is a well-respected magazine that covers music, culture, and entertainment, but it admitted to many missteps in the publication of its "A Rape on Campus" story.

CHAPTER 4

UNCOVERING THE TRUTH

Stories such as "Jimmy's World" and "A Rape on Campus" serve as cautionary examples of instances where publications failed to adequately verify the accuracy of their stories. More often, however, investigative journalism performs a public service by uncovering abuses such as illegal activities or corruption by people in power. Investigative news articles generally draw on multiple sources that corroborate the details of the story, such as documents and public records along with interviews of people involved in the case. Reporters frequently uncover facts that have been concealed.

This type of journalism exists to serve the public good. In many cases, the investigations uncover wrongdoing by people and organizations in positions of power. Publication of the story may contribute to their being held accountable for their actions.

CHILD SEX ABUSE EXPOSÉ

For over three decades starting in the 1960s, John J. Geoghan, a Catholic priest in Boston, abused children. The archdiocese of Boston knew, but instead of turning Geoghan over to the police when allegations were made—or when the priest himself admitted to abusing children—church leadership sent him for treatment and then reassigned him to new parishes. Members of these new parishes were not told about the allegations made against Geoghan.

All of this was discovered by investigative reporters at the *Boston Globe*. The Spotlight Team, reporters Matt Carroll, Sacha Pfeiffer, and Michael Rezendes, and editor Walter V. Robinson, spent months working on the first of its blockbuster articles. Although they planned a two-part series, starting with "Church Allowed

The Boston Globe Spotlight Team won the 2003 Pulitzer Prize for their articles about church leadership covering up abuse by priests and allowing them to continue to work with children.

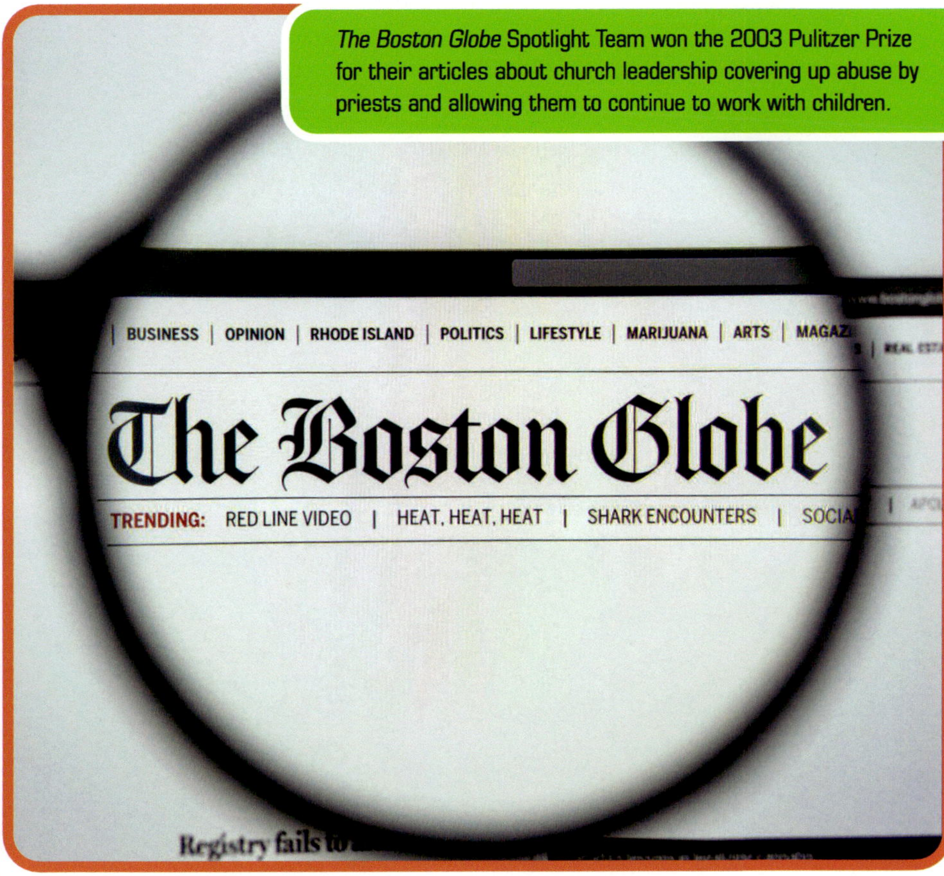

Abuse by Priest for Years" being published on January 6, 2002, and "Geoghan Preferred Preying on Poorer Children" published the following day, the team would go on to write 600 articles about abuse, cover-up, and corruption in the archdiocese.

For the investigation, the reporters interviewed abuse survivors and reviewed court documents from civil cases that were filed against Geoghan. These included depositions and personnel files for which the *Globe* had to file court motions to have them made public. Church officials would not answer questions about these stories.

Documentation can be critical for providing proof in an investigative journalism story. Journalists and citizens can use the Freedom of Information Act (FOIA) to obtain certain government documents.

The Spotlight Team was awarded the 2003 Pulitzer Prize for public service for these articles. The story of the team's investigation of the archdiocese was dramatized in the 2015 film *Spotlight*. The church reached settlements with some survivors. Cardinal Bernard Law resigned his post heading the archdiocese, and the Vatican began hearing cases of bishops who had been accused of either abusing children or covering up that abuse.

MAKING A DIFFERENCE ON CAMPUS

As they were preparing an article on their new principal, Amy Robertson, six student reporters at Pittsburgh High School in Pittsburgh, Kansas, discovered inconsistencies with the administrator's credentials. Through interviews and research, the young reporters raised doubts about Robertson's qualifications.

Their article, "District Hires New Principal," was printed in the *Booster Redux* on March 31, 2017, and provided details on Robertson's educational background. When interviewed by the students, Robertson said she had earned a bachelor of fine arts degree in theater from the University of Tulsa. The students contacted the University of Tulsa registrar's office and learned that the university never offered a bachelor of fine arts degree, only a bachelor of arts. The students also found that the university where Robertson received her master's and doctoral degrees was not accredited with the U.S. Department of Education. Four days after the article's publication, Robertson's resignation was announced at a school board meeting.

CORRUPTION IN CITY HALL

In July 2010, reporters Jeff Gottlieb and Ruben Vives posed this question to readers of the *Los Angeles Times*: "Is a City Manager Worth $800,000?" By reviewing city documents obtained under the California Public Records Act, the reporters discovered the exorbitant salaries paid to officials in Bell, California, a city with a population of 37,000 that, according to Gottlieb and Vives's article, had a per capita income that was about half that for the United States.

The reporters shared salaries for the city's top officials, contrasting what those in Bell made with what their counterparts in other cities were paid. The police chief, for example, received pay more than double that of New York City's police commissioner.

The *Times*' reports and state investigations revealed the level of corruption in Bell. City council members earned extra money by serving on agency boards that would meet for just one minute. Taxes were raised to cover the city manager's high salary. The city manager and other city officials would later be convicted of corruption. Gottlieb and Vives were awarded the 2011 Pulitzer Prize for public service for this coverage.

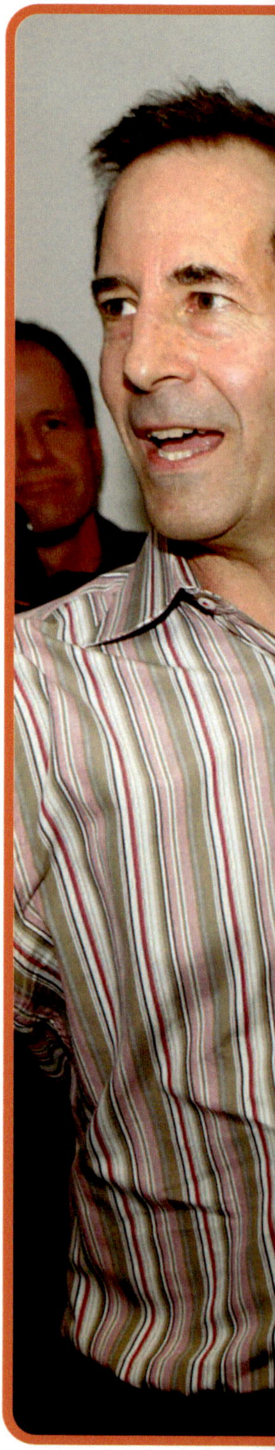

Los Angeles Times reporters Jeff Gottlieb and Ruben Vives won the Pulitzer Prize in 2011 for their reporting on government corruption in Bell, California.

The Pulitzer Prize is awarded annually in categories such as Public Service, Breaking News Reporting, Investigative Reporting, and Local, National, and International Reporting, among others.

EXAMINING "UNFOUNDED" ALLEGATIONS

Robyn Doolittle, a reporter for the *Globe and Mail,* spent 20 months investigating how police departments across Canada handled sexual assault allegations for the February 2017 feature series "Unfounded: Why Police Dismiss 1 in 5 Sexual Assault Claims as Baseless."

For the nine articles that made up "Unfounded," the *Globe and Mail* reached out to every police service in Canada and requested data from their unfounded cases. The paper received data from 873 of the country's more than 1,100 jurisdictions. Fifty-four complainants were interviewed about their experiences of reporting a sexual assault. The investigation not only found that one in five sexual assault allegations were determined unfounded, but that rates of unfounded cases varied drastically. Windsor, Ontario, for instance, had a 3 percent unfounded rate while Saint John, New Brunswick, had an unfounded rate of 51 percent.

Doolittle was honored at the National Newspaper Awards in 2018 with the prize for investigative journalism and was named journalist of the year. She was also awarded the 2018 Landsberg Award by the Canadian Journalism Foundation and Canadian Women's Foundation. Following the release of "Unfounded," police services across Canada reopened unfounded cases.

EXPOSING A PREDATOR

On August 4, 2016, the *Indianapolis Star* published "Out of Balance," an investigation that detailed how

Dr. Larry Nassar worked with USA Gymnastics from 1986 until 2015. Over 300 people have made allegations that they were sexually abused by Nassar.

USA Gymnastics covered up sexual misconduct and abuse allegations against its coaches. That morning, "Out of Balance" reporters Marisa Kwiatkowski, Mark Alesia, and Tim Evans received an email from Rachael Denhollander, a former gymnast, in which she revealed that the team doctor, Larry Nassar, had molested her under the guise of medical treatment.

Denhollander filed a complaint against Nassar with Michigan State University Police shortly after contacting the *Indianapolis Star* reporters. She agreed to be interviewed and identified for a new article, "Former USA Gymnastics Doctor Accused of Abuse," published in the paper in September 2016. The article alleged that USA Gymnastics knew about complaints against the doctor and did not adequately supervise him.

Nassar eventually pleaded guilty to criminal sexual conduct and federal child pornography charges. In 2018, at his sentencing, over 150 women shared their testimony about being abused by Nassar. The judge issued a sentence of 175 years in prison.

Newspapers serve as a crucial watchdog for the public interest, but traditional for-profit newspapers are in decline. In some places, nonprofit news outlets have emerged to fill niches left by the loss of traditional media. Nonprofit news organizations, which are funded by donors, come in many different sizes and specialties. ProPublica, for example, is a national nonprofit news outlet founded in 2007 that pursues investigative journalism. Kaiser Health News, launched in 2009, focuses on health care issues. There are also state and local nonprofit news organizations. In some cases, for-profit news outlets have managed to survive by converting to nonprofit status. In 2022, the Institute for Nonprofit News listed over 360 member organizations across the country, representing a growing alternative option to the fake news found on social media.

LIES AND SICKNESS

In 2020, the COVID-19 pandemic swept across most of the world, causing a public health crisis and transforming everyday life for ordinary people. An unprecedented wave of disinformation followed in the wake of the virus. Fake news was spread on the origins of Covid and whether it represented a genuine health threat. Disinformation stories questioned mortality rates and touted unproven cures. After vaccines were developed, fake news reports cast doubt on their safety and contributed to vaccine hesitancy. People's attitudes on measures such as lockdowns, restrictions on gatherings, and wearing face masks were affected by disinformation.

The Department of Homeland Security recommended relying on trusted sources such as the Centers for Disease Control (CDC) and state and local health departments, and warned against sharing stories on social media unless their accuracy had been verified. But official policy could change by the week or even day to day due to improved scientific understanding of Covid. People were left confused about where to turn for accurate information.

In 2021, the Pulitzer Prize awards reflected the media's achievements in clarifying the Covid crisis. The *New York Times* won the Public Service award for its Covid coverage. The winners of the awards for Explanatory Reporting and Feature Photography also addressed Covid.

Emilio Morenatti of the Associated Press won the 2021 Pulitzer Prize in Feature Photography for photographs of elderly patients in Spain struggling with the Covid crisis. Shown here is an artist's rendering of a Corona virus under a microscope.

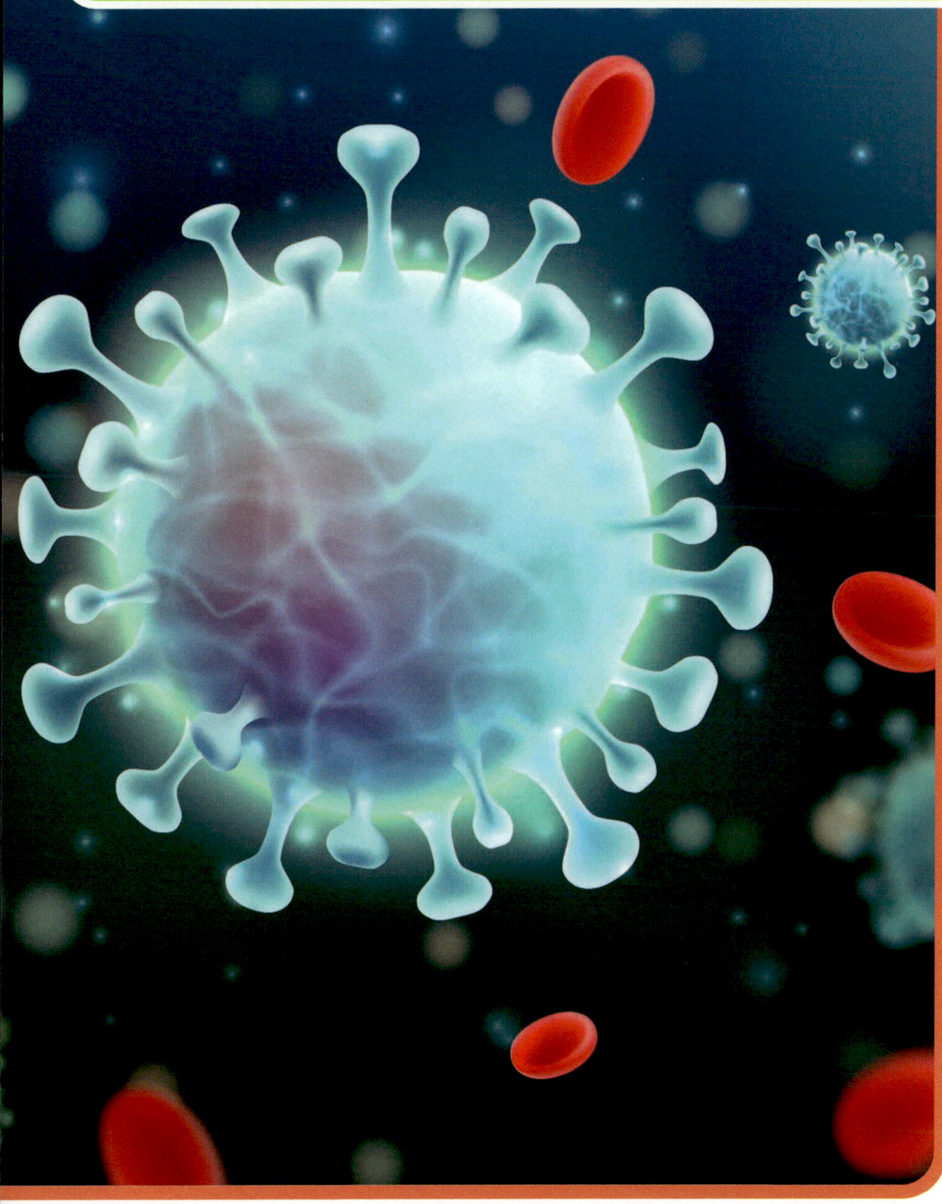

CHAPTER 5

INFORMATION EVERYWHERE

If you read a news story today, you're probably accessing it on a digital device. That's one of the findings of a 2021 poll by the Pew Research Center. Eighty-six percent of respondents reported that they sometimes accessed news on a smartphone, tablet, or computer. By contrast, 68 percent got their news through television, 50 percent through radio, and 32 percent from print media. Among digital device users, 68 percent accessed news through news websites or apps, 65 percent from search engines, and 53 percent through social media. Americans over the age of 50 are more likely to get their news through television than online, whereas younger Americans far prefer digital devices. Respondents between the ages of 18 and 29 were most likely to turn to social media for news on their devices, while older age groups preferred news websites or apps.

Among social media news consumers, the largest number (36 percent) turned to Facebook, followed by YouTube (23 percent) and Twitter (15 percent). Users don't necessarily trust social media as news—59 percent reported that they consider the news received on social media to be inaccurate.

Even if many people aren't fooled by fake news, disinformation can still have real consequences, as the people at the Comet Ping Pong pizza restaurant in Washington, D.C., learned on December 4, 2016.

The internet connects people instantly to breaking news stories, but make sure that you get your news from a reliable source.

FOOLED BY FAKE NEWS

Throughout her campaign for the presidency, Hillary Clinton faced criticism for her use of a private email server and potential mishandling of classified information during her time as secretary of state. She was also investigated by the Federal Bureau of Investigation (FBI), with then agency-head James Comey recommending that no criminal charges be filed against Clinton in July 2016.

Three months later, while investigating a case involving the husband of one of Clinton's top aides, Comey announced the FBI would reopen its investigation into Clinton. On the evening of that announcement, according to a timeline researched by Amanda Robb (with additional reporting by Aaron Sankin, Laura Starecheski, Michael Corey, Jaime Longoria, and Jasper Craven) for a November 2017 *Rolling Stone* article, a post was made on Facebook alleging that the presidential candidate, her husband, and several of their associates were involved in child abuse and trafficking. Similar posts appeared that day on message boards and in Facebook groups and were soon shared on Twitter.

The fake news story that became known as Pizzagate spread online over the course of five weeks. More fabricated and sensational details were added as the story spread. The narrative that eventually gained the attention of widely followed pundits like Alex Jones of Infowars was that Clinton and her associates were trafficking and abusing children who were being held captive in the basement of Comet Ping Pong.

U.S. presidential candidate Hillary Clinton was targeted by numerous conspiracy theories during her 2016 candidacy, including the Pizzagate claim that she was involved in child sex trafficking.

A man from North Carolina, Edgar Maddison Welch, heard the story on one of Jones's broadcasts and felt compelled to take action. Heavily armed with firearms and a knife, he entered the restaurant and searched the kitchen and back rooms, shooting out a lock during his invasion. Welch was sentenced to four years in prison and ordered to pay restitution for damage he did to the restaurant. No one at the restaurant was hurt in the incident. The Pizzagate conspiracy is still being spread online.

Contrary to conspiracy theory claims, Edgar Welch did not find any children being held captive in the basement when he stormed the Comet Ping Pong pizzeria in December 2016.

REGULATING FAKE NEWS OFFENDERS

Many Americans consider fake news a real threat. In 2019, a poll found that 39 percent of Americans believed that the government should restrict false information online. By 2021, that number had risen to 48 percent. Even more people believed that technology companies should take steps to curb disinformation.

The proposal to regulate fake news raises problematic ideological issues. Free speech is a constitutional right, and oversight of social media could limit freedom of information. Opponents of regulation assert that any government agency would be biased against certain political viewpoints.

In 2022, the European Union passed landmark legislation requiring tech companies to regulate material on their platforms. They will be required to remove content such as hate speech and terrorist propaganda. Other countries will be watching to see whether the measure succeeds in reining in fake news.

SPOOFING THE NEWS

In addition to the fake news, scandals, rumors, and hoaxes trying to get our attention, humor and satire are also in the mix. Sometimes, these are confused with real news. On television, *The Daily Show* has produced exaggerated, satirical segments that mimic actual news reports (and feature real people) while also commenting on true current events since its debut in 1996.

The Beaverton is a television show and website that features fictional stories that are inspired by news and current events in Canada. The show debuted in 2016, one day after the U.S. presidential election and six years after the website's launch. On television, segments have covered topics ranging from Canadian political figures to viral trends (such as the Tide Pod Challenge) to global conflict. Each is presented in the style of national evening broadcasts, but episodes are filled with exaggerated quotes and data. Online, *The Beaverton* covers the same topics as newspapers do, from national news to sports and culture. Its headlines include "Report: There Are a Bunch of Cities Outside Toronto with Their Own Streets and Buildings and Stuff," "Referee Reverses Call After Man Yells at TV Loud Enough," and "STUDY: TV Show Made for Teens Exclusively Consumed by Mid-Thirties Viewers."

Like the broadcast news shows it parodies, Canadian satire series *The Beaverton* features anchors, correspondents, and sports reporters, who are played by actors and comedians.

Though aspects of its stories are false, the people behind *The Beaverton* show and website are quick to point out that what they produce is not fake news. Satire exists to draw attention to social issues even as it makes people laugh, and it does not claim to be factually accurate.

The writers and editors behind *The Onion* have voiced similar frustration. Founded in 1988 as a print publication, the now web-only satirical publication features send-ups of current news and everyday life. Headlines have included "Exclusive TSA Pre-Check Allows Passengers to Fly Without Waiting for Airplane," "Dad Doesn't Trust the Fish Here," and "Trump Dismisses Trump as a Distraction." Though created to be humorous and satirical, sometimes *The Onion's* stories get taken seriously, like when a 2012 article naming North Korean dictator Kim Jong-Un "Sexiest Man Alive" was picked up as real news by China's *People's Daily*. The editors and writers at *The Onion* emphasize that the site's stories are not created to be taken as fact.

Although *The Onion* does not report real news, it can convey pointed commentary on society through its stories. For example, when a mass shooting occurs in the United States, the publication runs a brief story with the headline "'No Way to Prevent This,' Says Only Nation Where This Regularly Happens." As of 2022, *The Onion* had run the story 24 times since the original version in 2014. The recurring story, with the text nearly identical in every case, highlights the nation's failure to address gun violence.

CHAPTER 6

REJECTING FAKE NEWS

In 2017, a user posting as "Q" made the claim that the government, media, and big business is controlled by Satan worshippers who operate a child sex trafficking ring. These statements form the core of the elaborate conspiracy theory that has become known as QAnon. Eventually, according to the theory, "the Storm" will arrive when Trump will defeat the elites. The posts quickly spread through social media and grew in popularity.

QAnon has spread from the internet into the real world. QAnon followers participated in the January 6, 2021, attack on the U.S. Capitol. Politicians have promoted QAnon theories. The FBI designated QAnon a domestic terrorism threat in 2019.

According to a 2022 poll, 16 percent of the population of the United States—about 44 million people—responded that they agreed with QAnon views. Regardless of political affiliation, most QAnon followers trusted fringe media outlets. These people were five times as likely to believe in QAnon theories than consumers of mainstream media sources.

Social media has helped bring the world together. It allows us to stay in touch with distant family and friends, build new communities around shared interests, and gain awareness of important issues. Social media, though, can also narrow our worlds, confining us to spaces where everyone we interact with shares our viewpoints and ideals. Users can isolate themselves from diverse perspectives on issues. In this way, social media can contribute to tribalism, in which people associate themselves with certain beliefs and reject anyone who doesn't subscribe to their viewpoints.

Fake news and disinformation can thrive in this insular environment. For example, we may still share an inaccurate article if it supports a belief we have—a tendency called confirmation bias. Treating articles like this with caution is one way to help ease the spread of fake news.

Some rioters who stormed the U.S. Capitol on January 6, 2021, were QAnon promoters, including Jake Angeli, the "QAnon Shaman," who was among the first to enter the building.

FIGHTING DISINFORMATION

News consumers have a responsibility to stop the spread of fake news and disinformation. Social media companies are also stepping up and working on solutions for this issue. Facebook has introduced a number of plans and initiatives with the goal of making it more difficult for disinformation to flow throughout its network.

In the aftermath of the 2016 U.S. presidential election, Facebook faced criticism for the way the platform was used to spread inaccurate or fabricated information.

In April 2017, Adam Mosseri, vice president of news feeds at Facebook, shared on the company's blog three key areas it would be addressing in its fight against what Facebook terms "false news." Those key areas include:

- Disrupting economic incentives, meaning to prevent posters from making money by spreading fake stories
- Building new products, meaning to develop or improve tools on the network to keep fake stories out of users' news feeds
- Helping people make more informed decisions, meaning to find ways to give users more information about the stories they're reading on Facebook

This plan is ongoing at the company and has been integrated into its community standards. In 2020, Facebook banned QAnon accounts, and the company moved more aggressively against QAnon promoters following the January 6, 2021, attack on the Capitol. During the pandemic, Facebook took steps toward limiting Covid and vaccine misinformation.

Company efforts like these spread to its other brands. In 2018, Facebook-owned Instagram announced that it would be providing users with more information about accounts with large audiences. This includes when the account started and where the account is based as a way for followers to check an account's legitimacy.

KNOWING THE FACTS

Verified facts are a powerful antidote to misinformation. Researching every questionable article that comes your way, though, would be time-consuming and intensive. A number of individuals and organizations have stepped in to serve as fact-checkers for the internet, creating easily searchable sites web users can turn to when confronted with potentially false information, including those listed here.

Snopes (snopes.com) describes itself as "the internet's definitive fact-checking resource." The site researches and validates a wide range of internet content, from political news to viral memes. Snopes details its fact-checking methodology online, which includes reviewing the claim in question with the original source and independent experts. All fact-checks are reviewed by at least one editor before being posted to Snopes.com.

David Mikkelson launched the fact-checking resource Snopes in 1994. The site got its start investigating and debunking urban legends, hoaxes, and folklore.

PolitiFact (politifact.com) is a nonpartisan fact-checking organization owned by the nonprofit Poynter Institute for Media Studies that launched in 2007. The site checks specific statements made by politicians and notable figures for accuracy. It then uses its research—which includes on-the-record interviews and reviews of original documentation—to rate the statements on its Truth-O-Meter. The top rating a statement can receive from the site is "True," which the site describes as "accurate and there's nothing significant missing." PolitiFact.com's lowest rating is "Pants on Fire," which the site describes as "not accurate and makes a ridiculous claim."

The *Washington Post* originally launched its Fact Checker column in 2007 as part of its coverage of the 2008 U.S. presidential campaign. The column became a permanent feature for the paper in 2011. The Fact Checker (washingtonpost.com/news/fact-checker) focuses on newsworthy statements made by politicians, political candidates, diplomats, and interest groups. False statements are rated based on "The Pinocchio Test," named for the fairy tale character whose nose grew when he told a lie. They range from "One Pinocchio," which is given to statements that are mostly true, to "Four Pinocchios," which is given to what the site describes as "whoppers." A "Bottomless Pinocchio" rating is given to statements previously rated with three or four Pinocchios that has been repeated at least twenty times. The Fact Checker describes itself as bipartisan but acknowledges for readers the partisan nature of the statements it reviews.

BECOMING A SAVVY NEWS CONSUMER

Fact-checking sites are a quick resource for verifying if a story you have seen online is true. The web also offers tools to help you develop your own news judgment and become a smart consumer of information. Informed users are less likely to spread false, fabricated, or misleading information.

Sarah Blakeslee, a librarian with the Meriam Library at California State University, Chico, created the CRAAP Test in 2004 to help student researchers evaluate sources found online. The test can also be applied for judging the accuracy of news stories. CRAAP stands for currency (when the information was published), relevance (how the information relates to your needs), authority (who the source is for this information), accuracy (that the information is valid and verifiable), and purpose (why the information is being shared).

In school, we learn about the Five Ws and One H—who, what, when, where, why, and how—as questions to consider in research projects. Journalists follow this pattern in their investigations, adding in a sixth W—who cares—to give their stories relevance for readers. These questions can also be helpful tools to use when evaluating the accuracy of the news you're reading.

In its "Authentication 101—Tip Sheet," MediaSmarts used the Five Ws to create questions to ask for help in recognizing false content online: "What kind of false content should I watch out for? Why is it being spread around? Who is spreading it? Do they have a good track

In 2022, a global survey conducted by Cision found that journalists considered fighting accusations of fake news to be among their greatest challenges.

record for accuracy? When did it start spreading? Where else can I find out if something is real?"

Think about questions you can ask when reading news stories that will help you judge the accuracy of the event or statements being covered. You might wonder who the source for this information is, what the point of view of the publisher is, when the events in the article happened, where else this event is being covered, why the story is being covered, how the publication learned about the events, and who cares that this event happened.

On the Media is a weekly radio program and podcast produced by public radio station WNYC. It investigates how the press covers major issues. On its September 20, 2013, episode, the program introduced the "Breaking News Consumer's Handbook." This resource offers news viewers, readers, and listeners, in the words of the program, "some tips for how, in the wake of a big, tragic story, you can sort good information from bad." The program released over 20 handbooks that offer advice on how to analyze and critique news coverage of topics, including election polls, protests, and storms.

You can also expand your own awareness of different types of media sources. Too many people isolate themselves from diverse perspectives by consuming only news that conforms to their own ideologies. Check out the broadcast news on both CNN and Fox. Read the op-eds in the *New York Times* as well as the *Wall Street Journal*. Try out different types of news—instead of using the same app every time you read the headlines, check out YouTube or TikTok. Browse some podcasts and look into whether there are any new publications or outlets that match your interests.

Fake news and disinformation can be frustrating and even frightening, but becoming a savvy consumer of the news can be a rewarding and even enjoyable process. Don't passively accept every media story you encounter. Bring a skeptical, reflective, and engaged attitude to your media consumption. If you doubt the accuracy of a story, do some background research on the news source and the content of the article. Be aware of your own biases and wary of news pieces that confirm your biases too closely. Take a moment to confirm that you're confident in the story before you share it on social media. Media literacy is an important skill in today's connected and conflicted world, and recognizing fake news can help you evaluate the pressing issues at stake in society today.

10 GREAT QUESTIONS TO ASK TO BECOME A BETTER JUDGE OF NEWS

1. Has the person who shared this article with me shared fake or misleading articles in the past?

2. How reliable are the writers and news sources?

3. Can this news be corroborated, and are there photos, videos, or audio recordings to support the story?

4. Who is quoted as a witness or expert in the article?

5. Does the article align too closely with my biases?

6. Does the news outlet post a code of ethics or an editorial policy that describes its standards of reporting?

7. What are some reliable fact-checking sites on the internet?

8. Where can I find a guide to bias in news sources?

9. Are there any nonprofit news outlets covering my region, or that specialize in topics I'm interested in?

10. What news sources provide reliable information on current issues such as election news, the COVID-19 pandemic, and climate change?

GLOSSARY

archdiocese A territory overseen by an archbishop for the Catholic Church.

bias The favoring of one side of an argument over another.

bipartisan Involving cooperation between two political parties that normally oppose each other.

censorship The prevention of the publication or release of content that is considered objectional.

complainant One who complains or makes the complaint in a legal action.

fabricate To create false details or information that is presented as true.

fact An objectively verifiable piece of information.

freedom The ability to act without restrictions.

hoax A purposefully spread faked event or piece of information.

journalism The act of providing a detailed, factual, objective description of news events for distribution to the public.

libel A written defamatory statement.

media The general term for print, audio, video, and web news and entertainment outlets.

ombudsman A member of a newspaper staff who independently investigates issues at the publication brought up by editors or readers.

opinion A personal judgment or view on an issue or piece of information.

press A general term for print, audio, video, and web news organizations.

retraction The withdrawal of previously published content because of factual errors, plagiarism, or misleading statements.

right A legally protected act or action, such as voting.

satire The use of humor, irony, or exaggeration to make a point.

slander A spoken defamatory statement.

source An individual, report, research, or other material used for background in reporting a story.

FOR MORE INFORMATION

AMERICAN CIVIL LIBERTIES UNION (ACLU)

125 Broad Street, 18th Floor
New York, NY 10004
(212) 549-2500
Website: www.aclu.org
Facebook and Twitter: @ACLU
The ACLU defends the civil liberties guaranteed by the Constitution, including free speech and privacy in technology.

THE CANADIAN JOURNALISM PROJECT (A PROJECT OF CARLETON UNIVERSITY SCHOOL OF JOURNALISM)

J-Source at Ryerson University
350 Victoria Street
Room 4302C, River Building
Toronto, ON M5B 2K3
Canada
Website: j-source.ca
Facebook and Twitter: @jsource
Launched in 2007, the donor-supported Canadian Journalism Project provides resources such as news, research, commentary, and advice to journalists and students.

COMMON SENSE

San Francisco Headquarters
699 Eighth Street, Suite C150
San Francisco, CA 94103
(415) 863-0600
Website: www.commonsense.org
Facebook: @commonsensemedia
Twitter: @commonsense
Common Sense reviews and researches the media and technology used by kids. Common Sense Education (https://www.commonsense.org/education/) provides educational resources to empower kids to become savvy digital citizens.

FACTCHECK.ORG

202 S. Thirty-Sixth Street
Philadelphia, PA 19104
Website: www.factcheck.org
Facebook: @factcheck.org
Twitter: @factcheckdotorg
A nonprofit, nonpartisan project of the Annenberg Public Policy Center of the University of Pennsylvania, FactCheck.org monitors the accuracy of statements made by politicians with the goal of increasing public knowledge and understanding.

FREEDOM FORUM

9893 Brewers Court
Laurel, MD 20723
(202) 292-6100
Website: www.freedomforum.org
Facebook: @FirstAmendmentForAll
Instagram and Twitter: @1stforall
The Freedom Forum works to raise awareness of five freedoms guaranteed by the First Amendment.

POLITIFACT

c/o The Poynter Institute
801 Third Street South
St. Petersburg, FL 33701
(727) 821-9494
Website: www.politifact.com
Facebook and Twitter: @politifact
Owned by the Poynter Institute for Media Studies, the nonprofit PolitiFact checks the facts and rates the accuracy of statements made by U.S. politicians, government agencies, political organizations, and more.

SNOPES

Website: www.snopes.com
Facebook and Twitter: @snopes
Snopes is an independent fact-checking resource that investigates folklore, urban legends, and hoaxes, as well as misinformation and current events stories.

STUDENT PRESS LAW CENTER (SPLC)

1608 Rhode Island Avenue NW, Suite 211
Washington, D.C. 20036
(202) 785-5450
Website: splc.org
Facebook: @studentpress
Instagram: @studentpresslawcenter
Twitter: @splc
The nonprofit, nonpartisan SPLC functions as a resource providing information and legal assistance to high school and college journalists, educators, and advisers.

FOR FURTHER READING

Allen, John. *How Does Fake News Threaten Society?* San Diego, CA: ReferencePoint Press, 2020.

Cornell, Kari A. *Fake News*. San Diego, CA: ReferencePoint Press, 2020.

Hand, Carol. *Everything You Need to Know About Fake News and Propaganda*. New York, NY: Rosen Young Adult, 2018.

Leavitt, Amie Jane. *Digital Ethics: Safe and Legal Behavior Online*. New York, NY: Rosen Publishing, 2019.

Machajewski, Sarah. *American Freedoms: A Look at the First Amendment*. New York, NY: PowerKids Press, 2018.

Miller, Michael. *Fake News: Separating Truth from Fiction*. Minneapolis, MN: Twenty-First Century Books, 2019.

New York Times Editorial Staff. *Fake News: Read All About It*. New York, NY: New York Times Educational Publishing, 2019.

New York Times Editorial Staff. *Hacking and Data Privacy: How Exposed Are We?* New York, NY: New York Times Educational Publishing, 2019.

New York Times Editorial Staff. *Net Neutrality: Seeking a Free and Fair Internet*. New York, NY: New York Times Educational Publishing, 2019.

Nieuwland, Jackson. *Coping with Social Media Anxiety*. New York, NY: Rosen Young Adult, 2018.

INDEX

A

B

C

J

L

M

N

P

Q

ABOUT THE AUTHOR

ROBIN BAUSER has written numerous books for children and young adults, including titles addressing constitutional rights and current events issues affecting teens. She remains a fan of print magazines and newspapers as well as online news sources. Bauser lives in Chicago.

PHOTO CREDITS

Photo Credits: Cover, YAKOBCHUK VIACHESLAV/Shutterstock.com; Cover, pp. 1, 3-80 STUDIO DREAM/Shutterstock.com; Cover, p. 1 HIGOOD/Shutterstock.com; p. 5 https://commons.wikimedia.org/wiki/File:Johannes_Gutenberg.jpg; p. 6 Jan Schneckenhaus/Shutterstock.com; p.9 Andrew Hamilton defending John Peter Zenger in court, 1734-5]; p. 11 Stephen Coburn/Shutterstock.com; p. 13 pryzmat/Shutterstock.com; p. 15 Thomas Hengge/Shutterstock.com; p. 17 Billion Photos/Shutterstock.com; p. 18 https://commons.wikimedia.org/wiki/File:Nellie_Bly3.jpg; p. 20 https://commons.wikimedia.org/wiki/File:HEARST,_WILLIAM_RANDOLPH_LCCN2016858735.jpg; p. 23 Gorodenkoff/Shutterstock.com; p. 25 Alexander Khitrov/Shutterstock.com; p. 25 (inset) https://en.wikipedia.org/wiki/File:Pulitzer_Prizes_(medal).png; p. 26 BlurryMe/Shutterstock.com; p. 29 jdwfoto/Shutterstock.com; p. 31 Nicole Glass Photography/Shutterstock.com; p. 33 https://commons.wikimedia.org/wiki/File:ExxonMobil,_Polderdijkweg_foto_4.JPG; p. 35 https://commons.wikimedia.org/wiki/File:Steve-Coll-2017.jpg; p. 37 360b/Shutterstock.com; p. 39 II.studio/Shutterstock.com; p. 40 giggsy25/Shutterstock.com; p. 43 Katie Falkenberg/ASSOCIATED PRESS; p. 44 wellphoto/Shutterstock.com; p. 46 REUTERS / Alamy Stock Photo; p. 49 Fotomay/Shutterstock.com; p. 51 insta_photos/Shutterstock.com; p. 53 https://commons.wikimedia.org/wiki/File:Hillary_Clinton_(30464591050).jpg; p. 54 https://commons.wikimedia.org/wiki/File:Comet_Ping_Pong_Pizzagate_2016_01.jpg; p. 56 musgraphic/Shutterstock.com; p. 59 Johnny Silvercloud/Shutterstock.com; p. 60 askarim/Shutterstock.com; p. 62 Michael Vi/Shutterstock.com; p. 65 Microgen/Shutterstock.com.